DURING WORLD WAR II

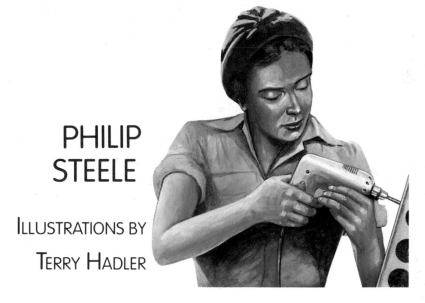

PHILIP
STEELE

ILLUSTRATIONS BY

TERRY HADLER

new
DISCOVERY
B·O·O·K·S
New York

Maxwell Macmillan Canada
Toronto

Maxwell Macmillan International
New York • Oxford • Singapore • Sydney

First American publication 1993 by New Discovery Books, Macmillan Publishing
Company, 866 Third Avenue, New York, NY 10022
Maxwell Macmillan Canada Inc., 1200 Eglinton Avenue East, Suite 200, Don Mills,
Ontario M3C 3N1

Macmillan Publishing Company is part of the Maxwell Communication Group of
Companies.

First published in Great Britain by Zöe Books Limited, 15 Worthy Lane, Winchester,
Hampshire SO23 7AB

A ZOË BOOK

Devised and produced by
Zöe Books Limited
15 Worthy Lane
Winchester
Hampshire SO23 7AB
England

Printed in Italy
Design: Julian Holland Publishing Ltd
Picture research: Victoria Sturgess
Illustrations: Terry Hadler
Production: Grahame Griffiths

10 9 8 7 6 5 4 3 2 1

Library of Congress Cataloging-in-Publication Data
Steele, Philip, 1948–
    Over 50 years ago : in Europe during World War II/ Philip Steele; illustrations by
Terry Hadler.
        p. cm. — (History detective)
    Includes index.
    Summary: Describes what life was like during World War II in Europe and the
devastation resulting from it.
    ISBN 0-02-786886-9
    1. World War, 1939-1945—Europe—Juvenile literature. I. Hadler, Terry, ill. II. Title.
III. Title: Over fifty years ago. IV. Title: In Europe during World War II. V. Series.
D743.7.S74   1993
940.53—dc20   92-40173

Photographic acknowledgments

The publishers wish to acknowledge, with thanks, the following photographic sources:

6 The Hulton-Deutsch Collection; 7,11t Rijksinstituut voor Oorlogsdocumentatie; 11b
Peter Newark's Military Pictures; 14t Rijksinstituut voor Oorlogsdocumentatie;
14b,17,18 Topham Picture Source; 19 Peter Newark's Military Pictures; 20/21 The Tate
Gallery, London; 22 Topham Picture Source; 23 The Hulton-Deutsch Collection; 26 The
Trustees of the Imperial War Museum, London; 27 Magnum (Franck)

Cover inset Magnum (Rodger)

CONTENTS

Y ou have lost your mother and father. Your home has been burned. Everywhere there are soldiers. With other refugees you escape from your village, but there are fighter planes overhead. Hungry and exhausted, you hide in a ditch....

This was the story of many thousands of European children during World War II. In 1939 German troops invaded Czechoslovakia. Soon their tanks were rolling westward into Belgium and France, northward into the Netherlands, Denmark, and Norway, and eastward into Poland, and the Soviet Union, and south into Yugoslavia and Greece.

For six long years Europe was torn apart by fighting. Life would never be the same again.

The war started in Europe, but it soon spread around the world. Fifty-seven nations went to war. More than 50 million soldiers and civilians died, half of them in the Soviet Union. Axis troops included Germans and Italians, supported in Asia by Japan. They fought the Allies, which included U.S., Soviet, French, British, and Commonwealth forces.

5

Two Nazis place stickers on the window of a dress shop. The stickers warn shoppers not to buy goods at stores owned by Jewish people. During the 1930s German Jews were mistreated and attacked by Nazis. Their legal rights were taken away. Worse was to follow.

A fight for freedom

World War II was the bloodiest conflict in the history of the world. Bombers destroyed cities, killing innocent children. Millions of people were murdered in death camps. Why did this terrible war happen?

Historians might start their detective work in the year 1918. In that year another deadly conflict, World War I, came to an end. Germany had been defeated, and the nation was bitter and divided. The German government was forced to pay huge amounts of gold to the victors. People were poor, many were unemployed, and money lost all its value. There were armed risings by communists. Many Germans were afraid. Their fears were played upon by a ruthless politician who promised to make Germany strong again.

The politician's name was Adolf Hitler. Hitler led the new National Socialist German Workers' ("Nazi") Party. At first the Nazis had little support, but they beat up or murdered those who disagreed with them. Democrats, liberals, and socialists became afraid to speak their mind.

Hitler bullied, lied, and cheated his way to power. He was a violent racist who encouraged attacks on Jewish people. He also despised the peoples of eastern Europe. When Hitler attacked their lands in 1939, Britain and France could stand by no longer.

There were political parties in other countries who shared the Nazis' ideas. In Italy and in Spain parties called Fascists also ruled through violence and hatred. Some people in France, Britain, and the United States agreed with the Fascists' ideas. Many others, however, wanted to stop them.

The date is May 10, 1940. A Dutch newsstand displays the usual movie magazines and comics. But today people can only read the shocking headlines of the newspapers: "German troops cross the Dutch border — Belgium and Luxembourg also attacked — The Queen speaks to the nation."

Searching for the past

Discover as much as you can about the war period. Many wartime buildings still stand. What were they used for? Museums contain weapons, uniforms, documents, and archives. There are also radio recordings, films, books, diaries, and newspapers. Many people remember the war years. Ask them what life was like in those days.

HISTORY DETECTIVE

German "stormtroopers," supported by tanks and aircraft, swept across Europe. Hitler claimed that Germans needed Lebensraum, or "space to live," in eastern Europe.

IN THE FRONT LINE

In September 1939 the Polish army went to war with horses and lances against German tanks. It was a hopeless contest. Modern technology had completely changed the methods of warfare.

World War II saw the development of new and powerful tanks, fast fighter planes, dive-bombers, and deadly submarines. Radar was used to detect enemy aircraft. Scientists developed rocket-powered flying bombs. Troops were moved at high speed over long distances, supported by aircraft. As armies spread terror across Europe, the Germans called it blitzkrieg — "lightning war."

Some countries did not join in the war. These neutrals included Sweden, Switzerland, Ireland, Spain, and Portugal. They remained neutral. Other countries soon fell to the Axis powers. They had occupied most of Europe by the end of 1940. Paris was captured, and British troops had to be rescued from the French port of Dunkirk. Yet Britain remained free, thanks to the airmen who defended it against heavy German air attacks.

In 1941 Germany invaded the Soviet Union, and Japan attacked the United States fleet in the Pacific Ocean. The Axis forces were now fighting two giants — and Britain had two new and powerful allies.

Fighter pilots scramble to their planes during the Battle of Britain. The weeks of aerial warfare began on August 15, 1940. Pilots from occupied Europe and from the British Commonwealth fought alongside young British pilots.

Fighting men and women

Who fought in World War II? Some soldiers were professionals. They had volunteered to fight before the war started. Most troops were ordinary young men who had been "called up," or drafted.

Women played much greater roles than ever before. They worked as drivers, mechanics, nurses, and intelligence officers. In the Soviet air force some women flew in daring night raids over enemy lines.

Australians, New Zealanders, Africans, and Asians all fought with the Allies. U.S. and Canadian soldiers became familiar sights on the streets of London. They were joined by a growing band of soldiers who had fled from occupied Europe. There were Polish airmen,

Dutch sailors, and an army of Free French.

The Axis troops were joined by Fascist volunteers from other countries and by soldiers who had been forced to join the German army in eastern Europe. There were Finns, Hungarians, Romanians, Croats, and Ukrainians. Soldiers on both sides were captured and sent to prisoner of war camps. Some managed to escape. People who came from an enemy country, such as Germans living in Britain, were also held in internment camps. They were not allowed to travel freely.

Soldiers were not the only people to risk death in combat zones. Merchant ships carried goods on convoys between the United States, Britain, and the Soviet Union. Many ships were sunk by torpedoes, and their crews were killed.

Some of the most dangerous work in the war was carried out by members of the resistance. If discovered, they risked torture and death. This woman helped to produce an illegal newspaper in the Netherlands. News from the Allies was picked up on secret radios.

Truth or fiction?

In newspaper or film reports on both sides, every soldier was a hero and every battle a victory. Was this true? Why were mistakes or scandals covered up? News was censored. Some history books written after the war also distorted the truth. The history detective must try to find out what really happened.

WAFFEN-⚡⚡
EINTRITT NACH VOLLENDETEM 17. LEBENSJAHR

This German recruiting poster was printed in 1941. It was aimed at 17-year-olds and showed a heroic image of warfare. The reality was very different.

In occupied Europe many men and women fought a secret war. They were spies, members of the resistance, or fighters called partisans.

On September 6, 1942, the Soviets stopped the German advance at Stalingrad. During 1943 the United States took part in the bombing of Germany and the liberation of Italy. On June 6, 1944, 4,000 boats, 600 warships, 9,500 aircraft, and 176,000 Allied troops crossed the English Channel to attack the beaches of Normandy, in occupied France. D Day had arrived… and the tide of the war was turning.

This was the first total war in history. Civilians' lives, as well as those of the troops in the front line, were in danger. From the Soviet Union to the United States women worked long hours in factories. They made bombs, packed parachutes, or built aircraft. In Britain and in Germany young women worked on farms, helping to bring in the harvest. It was often exhausting work. British, French, and German civilians learned to fight fires or drive ambulances. Others checked the blackout — lights might be seen by enemy bombers. When an air raid was expected, wardens made sure that people took shelter. After a raid volunteers were needed to rescue survivors or provide food or drink. The cities of Europe became a battlefield

from which nobody could escape.
Only young, fit men were called up. Older men joined local defense groups, the home guard. By the end of the war Berlin was being defended by old men and young boys. In Britain some young men were ordered to work in the coal mines. In countries occupied by the Nazis, men were taken away to Germany as forced labor.

Bombing by both sides brought terror to ordinary people. In 1944 the dikes were bombed in the Dutch province of Zeeland. As the walls of earth crumbled, the sea flooded in over vast areas of farmland. Many people were drowned or made homeless.

Death from the skies

One sound can still strike fear into people who remember the war in Europe — the wailing sound of air-raid sirens.

At night the skies were crisscrossed by searchlights and lit up by antiaircraft fire and blazing buildings. Large barrage balloons floated above cities to prevent the approach of enemy aircraft. Public buildings were protected by walls of sandbags. To prevent shattering, windows were taped over.

Public air-raid shelters were built, and many people slept in cellars or subway stations. Small family shelters were built in gardens.

At the start of the war people were given gas masks. These strange-looking goggles would allow people to breathe if chemical weapons were used by the enemy. Luckily, they were never needed.

City dwellers were mostly affected by air raids, but country people across Europe also suffered. Bombs were dumped over villages, aircraft crash-landed, and tanks tore up fields. All signposts were removed in order to confuse enemy troops.

Many families from London went to the countryside during the summer. In 1940 trenches were dug in the fields to protect the children, as air battles raged overhead.

Many German cities were destroyed by Allied bombing raids. Fires raged and buildings collapsed. Many civilians were killed by bombs. People tried to carry on with their lives as normal.

Signs of warfare

Europe was scarred by World War II. For years empty bomb sites gaped in cities. Concrete gun emplacements can still be seen along coasts. Small forts stand in woods and fields. Unexploded bombs are still sometimes found today. Why were many places bombed? Were they the sites of docks, factories, or railways? What is a war memorial?

HISTORY DETECTIVE

From Italy to the Soviet Union, from Greece to France, millions were left homeless, injured, or dead. Ancient towns were reduced to rubble by the fighting. Soldiers returning home on leave did not recognize the streets where they had lived. Power stations and gas and water pipes were destroyed. On both sides people showed great bravery in rescuing or helping their neighbors.

Both sides wanted to make the enemy believe that they could not win the war. They bombed cities to destroy people's confidence, or morale. They knew that thousands of people would be killed.

In September 1940 Hitler began to bomb London and other British cities. These terrible raids became known as "the Blitz."

In turn the Allies bombed German cities. Cologne and Berlin were flattened, and Dresden burned like a fireball. About 130,000 people were killed and 400,000 were injured in Dresden in 1945.

15

In lands under German rule there was more to fear than bombs and tanks. A knock on the door could mean the arrival of the dreaded Nazi secret police, the gestapo. Many civilians were arrested, tortured, and executed. For Jewish people discovery by the Nazis meant death.

In Warsaw Jews were gunned down and their homes were burned. Others, along with Jews from all over Europe, were taken by train to horrific concentration camps in Germany and Poland. Here about six million Jews were starved to death or murdered in gas chambers.

Anne Frank in 1940

Wartime was hard for many children. City children in Britain were sent away, or evacuated, to the countryside, far from home.

Anne Frank wrote a diary during these frightening years. She was born in Germany in 1929. Her family was Jewish, so they fled to the Netherlands in 1933. When the Germans invaded, Anne's family hid in a secret room. In 1944 they were captured and taken to the death camp at Belsen.

These Polish farmers had to pull their own plow. There was no gas for a tractor, and the army had taken away their horses. All over Europe gasoline was strictly rationed. In France, cars were sometimes pulled by horses.

Wartime rations

Children who grew up during the war had never tasted a banana or an orange. Cookbooks suggested using powdered eggs and whale meat. Everyone was encouraged to grow their own food — "Dig for Victory" was one campaign in Britain. In Germany there were many ersatz ("substitute") foods. People drank "coffee" made from acorns. In the last months of the war the Dutch experienced a "Hunger Winter." A day's food supply was two slices of bread, two potatoes and half a beet. Some people ate tulip bulbs. Many died. Fuel was scarce throughout Europe, as coal and oil were used for the war effort. Furniture was made from cheap plywood. Clothing, too, had to be simple. Wartime governments controlled the supply of

As German troops withdrew from the Netherlands, the Dutch people were starving. Soon there was starvation in Germany itself. Soldiers fleeing from the Allied advance were lucky to find a bowl of warm soup.

Both American and British posters warned of the danger of "careless talk." If spies overheard gossip about troop movements, weapons factories, or secret plans, they would pass the information back to the enemy. Public information posters from both sides of the conflict tell us a great deal about everyday life in World War II.

goods. Books were issued containing ration coupons, which were handed to the shopkeeper before buying anything. Rationing was most severe in occupied Europe. Scarce goods, such as cigarettes or stockings, were sometimes sold illegally, on the black market.

People learned to put up with shortages and to survive great hardships. But they longed for an end to the war. Rationing continued into the 1950s.

Coupons and cards
Historians use all sorts of documents to make a picture of the past. There are British ration books and U.S. war bond certificates. There are party membership cards of Italian Fascists and Soviet Communists. There are French identity cards and German passes. Some of these were forged by spies or by prisoners of war. Why would they need them?

IMAGES OF WAR

Paintings by wartime artists can tell us about everyday life 50 years ago. The great British sculptor Henry Moore was an official war artist from 1940-1942. He drew pictures of Londoners sleeping in underground stations during the Blitz. The Nazis hated artists who painted in the modern style. They preferred "romantic" pictures painted in a realistic manner. German painters and architects who opposed the Nazis fled

to America and to the free countries of Europe during the 1930s. The Nazis publicly burned books of which they disapproved. The writers Thomas Mann and Bertolt Brecht soon joined the flood of refugees from Germany.

German orchestras played operas by Wagner (1813-1883). Music by Jewish composers was banned. The Russian composer Dmitri Shostakovich (1906-1975) wrote his Seventh Symphony in honor of the people who defended his homeland.

Finding some leisure time

Homes did not have television in the 1940s. For entertainment and for news, people went to movie theaters. Some of the films were romances or war adventures. They helped to keep people cheerful and hopeful. Both sides knew that this was very important.

At home, radio programs were very popular. The catchphrases of favorite comedians were known by everyone. Radio also served more serious purposes. It was used for broadcasting public information and for propaganda.

A German military band plays to French crowds during the occupation of Paris.

The world-famous comedian Charlie Chaplin made fun of Adolf Hitler in his 1940 film The Great Dictator.

The German singer and movie star Marlene Dietrich was opposed to the Nazis. She performed concerts for the Allied troops, singing the popular hit "Lili Marlene." Here she signs autographs for sailors of the Free French forces.

One German pop song, "Lili Marlene," became a hit with Allied troops and was recorded in English. Singers and movie stars visited the troops and put on shows. American GIs brought with them to Europe new music called "swing" and "boogie-woogie," and dances such as the jitterbug.

Picture magazines and newspapers told stories of the troops and the home front. They also showed photographs of famous movie stars in distant Hollywood.

Words from wartime

The language we speak is part of living history. Many words first used in World War II are still with us today. They include army slang, phrases from songs, slogans, and abbreviations. The word *GI*, for an American soldier, came from his uniform, which was "Government Issue." The word *blitz* is still used to describe any sudden or drastic attack.

HISTORY DETECTIVE

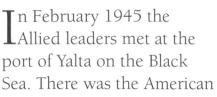

PEACE AT LAST

In February 1945 the Allied leaders met at the port of Yalta on the Black Sea. There was the American president Franklin Delano Roosevelt, who was to die just before the end of the war. There was the British prime minister Winston Churchill. He was a popular figure, whose "V" for Victory sign inspired hope through the grim years of war. Marshal Joseph Stalin, the cunning and ruthless leader of the Soviet Union, was also there.

Allied victory now seemed certain. In August 1944 the tanks of the Free French had led the Allies into Paris. In March 1945 the Allies, under the command of U.S. General Dwight D. Eisenhower, crossed the Rhine River. To the east the Soviet Red Army was sweeping across central Europe.

The retreating Germans blew up bridges to slow the Allied advance. Soon, however, the Soviet flag was flying over the ruins of Berlin, and American and Russian troops were meeting on the Elbe River.

All over liberated Europe crowds danced in the streets and wept for joy. Here American GIs join the crowds in Paris.

The troops come home

The war in Europe finally came to an end at 2:41 A.M. on May 7, 1945. The Fascist leader Benito Mussolini had been killed by Italian partisans in Milan. Adolf Hitler had shot himself in Berlin. Germany and Austria were now occupied by Allied troops, and Berlin was divided between the victors. The world was soon horrified to learn of the Nazi concentration camps, with their piles of dead and their few, pitiful survivors.

American troops now returned home from Europe. Thousands were packed on to ocean liners for the Atlantic crossing. They were welcomed home with flags and parades. Many GIs married women they had met in Europe during the war.

The war ended in bitterness. Leading Nazis were imprisoned. They were tried for war crimes and some were executed. In countries where the Germans had ruled, people who had helped them were shot. They were called collaborators. French women who made friends with German soldiers were attacked. Their heads were shaved by angry crowds.

In August the war in the Pacific ended after atomic bombs were dropped on Japan. For most Europeans, however, it was a happy time. Gradually the troops were sent home, or demobilized, and returned to their families. City lights shone again in Paris, Amsterdam, Oslo, and London.

The 40th anniversary of the D Day landings. The flags of the Allies are raised again on the beaches of Normandy. It was here that the liberation of Europe began.

Why study history?

One reason that we study the past is to learn lessons for the future. Hitler boasted that the peoples of northern European origin were better than any others. All he proved was that they were capable of very great evil. The true story of the concentration camps must never be forgotten. Yet the evils of fascism and racism do not belong to any one people or nation, or to any single time. Since the war new Fascists have appeared in Europe, South Africa, and the Americas.

There is only one possible tribute to the millions of ordinary Europeans — including many Germans, Austrians, and Italians — who made a stand against the tide of fascism. Never to let it happen again.

HISTORY DETECTIVE

27

1918	World War I comes to an end
1919	Treaty of Versailles: Germany loses territory and is forced to pay vast amounts to the victors
1922	Fascists march on Rome. Benito Mussolini becomes Italian prime minister.
1923	Adolf Hitler imprisoned in Germany
1933	Adolf Hitler becomes German chancellor. Nazis attack and murder opponents.
1934	Austrian chancellor Engelbert Dollfuss murdered by Nazis. Hitler becomes leader, or Führer, of Germany.
1935	Jews persecuted in Germany
1936	Civil war in Spain. Germany and Italy support the Spanish Fascists under General Franco. Axis pact between Germany and Italy.
1938	Germany invades Austria and makes it part of the German Empire, or *reich*. Britain and France make a pact with Hitler, granting Germany part of Czechoslovakia.
1939	Germany seizes rest of Czechoslovakia. Italy invades Albania. September 1: Germany invades Poland. September 3: Britain and France declare war on Germany. Nazi-Soviet Pact.
1940	Japan joins Axis powers. Germany invades Denmark, Norway, Belgium, the Netherlands, France. British army evacuated from French port of Dunkirk. Battle of Britain — British Royal Air Force defeats German Luftwaffe. Italy declares war on Allies and invades Greece.

1941	Germany invades Soviet Union. Japan attacks U.S. fleet at Pearl Harbor. U.S. declares war on Axis powers.
1942	Soviets defeat Germans at Stalingrad
1943	U.S. bombers join attack on Germany. Allied invasion of Italy.
1944	Allies liberate Rome and land in Normandy. In Germany an attempt to kill Hitler. Allies liberate Paris and Brussels, begin liberation of the Netherlands. Germans crush uprising in Warsaw. British troops land in Greece.
1945	Soviet troops liberate Warsaw. Allied summit conference at Yalta. Germany invaded by Allies. Death of Mussolini and Hitler. May 7: Germany surrenders. May 8: Victory in Europe (V-E Day). August 6: Atomic bombs dropped on Hiroshima and Nagasaki, in Japan. August 14: Japan surrenders, end of World War II. November 25: Opening of trials at Nuremberg — leading Nazis accused of war crimes.

For Further Reading

Aaseng, Nathan. *Cities at War: Paris*. New York: New Discovery Books, 1992.

Adler, David. *We Remember the Holocaust*. New York: Henry Holt & Co., 1989.

Ayer, Eleanor H. *Cities at War: Berlin*. New York: New Discovery Books, 1992.

Fyson, Nance L. *Growing Up in the Second World War*. North Pomfret, VT: Trafalgar Square, 1981.

Hanmer, Trudy. *Cities at War: Leningrad*. New York: New Discovery Books, 1992.

Klingeman, William K. *1941: Our Lives in a World on the Edge*. New York: HarperCollins, 1988.

Kronenwetter, Michael. *Cities at War: London*. New York: New Discovery Books, 1992.

Landau, Elaine. *We Survived the Holocaust*. New York: Franklin Watts, 1991.

Landau, Elaine. *Nazi War Criminals*. New York: Franklin Watts, 1990.

Landau, Elaine. *The Warsaw Ghetto Uprising*. New York: New Discovery Books, 1992.

Leckie, Robert. *Delivered from Evil: The Saga of World War II*. New York: HarperCollins, 1987.

Newton, David E. *Cities at War: Tokyo*. New York: New Discovery Books, 1992.

Sherrow, Victoria. *Cities at War: Amsterdam*. New York: New Discovery Books, 1992.

GLOSSARY

air raid: a bombing attack on ground targets by enemy aircraft

Allies: those countries that fought the Axis powers during World War II, including the United States, Britain, the Free French, and the Soviet Union

archives: a collection of public records, historical documents, photographs, or films

Axis: an alliance between Italy and Germany formed in 1936, later extended to include Japan

barrage balloons: large inflatables tethered by cables, designed to hinder air attack

black market: illegal trading during wartime

blackout: during the war all lights had to be concealed at night. This prevented enemy bombers finding targets

blitzkrieg: unexpected and violent attacks on the enemy

censor: to restrict information, or place an official ban on the free expression of ideas. During World War II newspaper articles and broadcasts were strictly censored, as were letters sent home by the troops.

collaborator: someone who works with the enemy; a traitor

communist: believing that industry and government should be controlled by the workers. The communist Soviet Union at first made a pact with Hitler but later fought the Nazis. Communist partisans fought in Greece, Italy, and Yugoslavia.

concentration camp: a guarded prison camp. The Nazis placed millions of Jews, Gypsies, political opponents, and homosexuals in brutal death camps.

D Day: the day on which the Allied liberation of occupied France began — June 6, 1944

demobilize: to disband the armed forces at the end of the war

democrat: somebody who believes in government by the people, usually through a system of fair elections. The Fascists were against democracy.

draft: to compel people to join the armed forces

evacuate: to move people away from danger

Fascist: somebody who believes that the state should have total control over the individual. The Italian Fascist party, founded in 1922, took its name from the *fasces*, the bundle of sticks that was a badge of state power in ancient Rome.

flying bomb: a powered, winged bomb that does not have to be dropped from an aircraft

Free French: French people who, led by General Charles de Gaulle, continued the fight against the Nazis

gas mask: a respirator or mask that filters the air breathed during a chemical attack

GI: a slang term for an American soldier

home guard: a reserve defense force such as the German Volksturm, set up to fight invading troops. Many of its members were elderly. The British home guard is fondly remembered as a "Dads" Army.

internment camps: places where many people had to live because, although they lived in a country, they were of "enemy" nationality. They could not travel around freely.

liberal: somebody who believes in individual freedom and civil rights; holding progressive views

liberation: the freeing of a country from oppressive rule or occupation

morale: confidence, enthusiasm, or high spirits

Nazi: a member of the racist National Socialist German Workers' Party (NSDAP) founded after World War I. It was neither socialist nor acting in the interest of German workers.

neutral: a country that does not enter military alliances or take part in a war

partisan: an irregular or guerrilla fighter attacking an army of occupation

prisoner of war (POW): a member of the armed forces captured by the enemy. An international agreement, the Geneva Convention, laid down rules for the treatment of POWs in captivity.

propaganda: information, often misleading, intended to gain support for one's own cause and to discredit that of the enemy

radar: a system of locating objects such as ships or aircraft by using radio waves (**RA**dio **D**etecting **A**nd **R**anging)

rationing: an official limit placed upon the supply of food, clothes, or other goods

resistance: a secret group of men and women who attack an army of occupation

socialist: believing in public ownership of industry. Many socialists and trade unionists were imprisoned and killed by the Nazis.

victor: the winner of a battle or war

war bond: a savings certificate issued by a government in order to raise money during wartime

war crime: a crime committed during wartime, such as the massacre of civilians or the killing of prisoners of war

INDEX

940.5   Steele, Philip.
STE
         Over 50 years ago in
         Europe.

$13.95

DATE			